MY LABYRINTH OF FIRE

The Poetry of A Tasmanian Manic Depressive

by

NED PICKERING

Copyright © 2025 by Ned Pickering

This is a work of fiction. Names, characters, businesses, places, events, and incidents are either the products of the author's imagination or used in a fictitious manner. Any resemblance to actual persons, living or dead, or actual events is purely coincidental.

ISBN: 978-0-646-72565-9

Publisher: Ned Pickering Arts

About the Author

Ned Pickering (b. 2001, Hobart, Tasmania) is a author, musician, and painter whose work is rooted in fire, sea, and the raw edges of the human mind. *My Labyrinth of Fire: The Poetry of a Tasmanian Manic Depressive* is his first collection of poetry, drawn from lived experience of manic depression and shaped by the island landscapes that raised him.

Outside poetry, Ned's creative life moves across disciplines. He has played traditional Irish fiddle for a decade — taught by his Dublin-born grandparents and refined through classical lessons, mentorship, and study of legendary players. His oil paintings reimagine Tasmania's coastlines in high-chroma, mosaic-like colours, and his fiction blends myth and grit, with a debut novella, *The Empress of Fire*, released in 2025 and an Australian epic-fantasy set to take the literary world by storm, *The Venator's Son: A Ballet of Blades*.

Through *Ned Pickering Arts*, he performs, paints, and writes as one practice, sharing stories of Tasmania's weather, wilderness, and inner storms. *My Labyrinth of Fire* stands as both testament and offering: art made in the blaze of struggle, carried out into the world.

For all those touched with fire

Table of Contents

About the Author iii

I. IGNITION 1
Perfect Disorder 2
Cultivate 3
Death 4
Turbulence 5

II. MASKS & SHADOWS 7
The Ball 8
Shades 9
Lost 10
Drowning 11
My Labyrinth of Fire 12

III. COLLAPSE 13
That Thrumming Bed 14
The In-between Place 15
Ripped Out Curtains 16
Touching the Intersection 17

IV. REVOLT & REVOLUTION 19
Down with the Skies 20

Euthymia 21
Beyond My Skin.. 22

V. THE LABYRINTH RETURNS 23
Pipedreams 24
Take Me 25
Corpses 26

VI. THE PRECIPICE 27
The Precipice 28

I.
Ignition

Perfect Disorder

And boom.

Colours again.

Everything in perfect disorder,
Soul cut loose, everything you look at turned sacred,

Fire.

Cultivate

How do we bring back the fire but
keep it from burning everything down?

I can't tame my fire.
I want to cultivate it and make it useful like a cooking fire,
But it always sneaks into a bonfire, and I get distracted with how
pretty it is.

What a mystery water is?
It seems to just fall out of the sky.

Death

Death is there,
Looking over your shoulder,
On the tip of your tongue,
In the bottom of your lungs.

Death is there,
Under that tree,
Rustling through the leaves,
In the pitch black of night.

Death is there,
Where you won't look,
In the missing sound,
The unfinished book.

Dogs bark,
Engines roar,
Doors close.

Shh — she's here.
"Who's she? — just say it."
"I don't know what waving your arms
around means — you're scaring me."

I had never been so afraid in all my life.

Turbulence

I said, "It's going to be too windy that day."
But I could never have imagined the turbulence.

I was possessed and ran away.

I felt the ocean looking back at me,
Breathing, swallowing, roiling in the dark.

I went in — boots, jeans and all.

I can't remember how I got out,
But I lost something in the waves.

Centipedes, spiders, snakes and bugs,
Every handhold to the way above.

I lost something in the waves.

# II.
# Masks & Shadows

The Ball

Faces, people, short and tall,
Should I even go at all?

Will it be quiet or it be loud?
How many names goes by the crowd?

Will I laugh while I cry?
Will they sing the truths in every lie?

Pretty people, cracks within,
All my masks have worn thin.

Shades

Death is standing outside my house.

He nods his brim as we leave.
Unseens eyes, behind his shades,
Cap and T-shirt,
A smile and wave.

Why do you loiter?
We're going away.

Why do you loiter?
When you're welcome to stay.

Lost

Lost in the forest,
Lost in the waves,
Lost in the colours,
My hand-painted graves.

Drowning

Hazy, lazy autumn day,
Colours came, washed away,
Help me, help me,
I can't say.

Drowning in the shades of grey.

My Labyrinth of Fire

Walls are burning,
Death's wound in desire,
How do I get out,
Of my labyrinth of fire?

III.
Collapse

That Thrumming Bed

Played along with like a child,
Until death came in uniforms.

Sitting cross-legged on the grass
Mum rolls me a cigarette awfully.

They lead me to that thrumming bed.

Suffocated by twenty helping hands,
A faceless crowd.

Held down,
Strapped up.

Jabbed.

I can't remember if I screamed, "They're killing me."

I can't remember a word I said.

The In-between Place

My chest-breaking vortex,
An impossible pouring — in and out at once,
Everything and nothing in perfect oxymoron,
Sets my sheets ablaze and soaks them through and through.

I want to return to the dreamscape.
I want to soar and swim in the sky.

I want to but I can't go.
Inside my bones it's setting fire to snow.

Where does it end?
When the sun kissed the sky forever goodbye?
When the wind dies away in the hills on the last day on earth?

Is this the end?
To gawk at every tree and shadow that fleets under their eaves?

Am I lost in the waves?
Trying to fix myself upon what is unfixable,
Desperately clawing my way up to see the intersection,
That place where sea and sky and stone meet.

The in-between place.

Ripped Out Curtains

I'll keep on singing till the day that I drop,
My voice is calling — can it find my flock?
These days I just let the wind rip the curtains,
Change is the constant, she told me, I'm certain.

I wear my halo like an invisible ring,
My angels watch me, they can't touch this thing.
Sometimes I'm swimming and it's hard to let go,
But you can't hold on to what you cannot know.

I read the forest from a single leaf,
It whispers things that you cannot speak.
I'll scream it out from the top of my lungs.
There's something listening way up above.
Change is the constant, she told, it's certain.
In the cold of night now I'm wishing for curtains.

I see the darkness — it sees me.
I kiss the shadows — they turn into trees.
Branches reaching, clawing, I see!
I give my hand out,
"Come and dance with me."

Change is the constant, I believe her, she's certain.
She's in the wind now and the ripped-out curtains.

Touching the Intersection

An eye in the sky,
A hole in my fingertip where I touched it — the space in-between.
Now this red lighter will never go out, and when it does it'll be my last breath.

The card-cutter cut himself from the deck.

Bodies tangled in the wheels,
Souls lost in the hills.

Burn all the lighters, cut all the bases,
Forget the right ones in a mosaic of faces.

Where you're going you won't need your red lighter.
Where you're going there's no use for purple and gold paint.

Where you're going there's no going.

IV.
Revolt & Revolution

Down with the Skies

Let them listen.
Let them come.
Let them hear the earth-shaking thrum.

Let them whisper.
Let them love.
Let them cling to what's above.

Wind back the hands,
Cut the earbuds,
Fill the mangled, broken beer-mugs.
Raise it up, this offering,
Find the lost, invisible ring.

Tear down the skies,
Burn all the seas,
Dissolve the land,
Upturn the trees.

Mountains will be mountains,
Seas will be seas.

The power lies in what you believe.

Euthymia

Mountains are mountains again,
Rivers are rivers,
The skies no longer burn,
The trees no longer claw.

What once was burning,
Is again raw,

Mountains will be mountains,
Seas will be seas,
Don't look too closely,
At the space in-between.

Beyond My Skin

Everything ignites again.

Skies ablaze as they should be,
Bursting gilded light turns everything it touches sacred.

The wind of change blows hard enough to knock me over.
It makes the sea roil and dance.

Wild and excited.

The mountain watches like a slumbering leviathan.

Skies trembling,
Seas trembling.

They are trembling beyond their skins.

V.
The Labyrinth Returns

Pipedreams

It's a pipedream.
Armchairs and stretched out silence.

A life free from the system by rite of
passion and fire between the fingers.

Some kind of magic.
A pipedream.

Isn't that where it always flows,
To keep the watchtower burning until the stones erode.

That signal home,
Even in the dark it glowed.

When the ferryman waved his lantern — an extension cord of wire,
His lonely boat, the branch of beachside tree,
That way out that I did conspire.

You cannot quench that kind of desire.

That's what the walls are made of in my labyrinth of fire.

How do I get out?
I still haven't a clue,
There is always sitting back, enjoying the view

Take Me

I was swimming in the sunset,
Higher than an angel, not one drop wet,
I was a general winning the war,
Blood on my hands and my enemies torn.

Mountains gave in,
Oceans un-poured.
The skies all burnt up, someone settled the score.

Screaming in the dark.
Hades.

Cigarettes, grass.
Stain me.

With the deep, deep dark,
Tame me.

Lay me down, strap me up.
Sedate me.

Break me down,
Jab me up.

Take me.

Corpses

A bleak awakening,
Mould still on the windows,
A shrouded sky.

No telling when it will go.

My clothes are like corpses on the floor,
Remnants, echoes, lying forlorn.
Soldiers sent off to the war.

The last line trembles.

It barely holds.

Only saved by neglect,
A fear and hope — the final stroke,
A pain so real and visceral.

The ferryman waves cheerfully.
"It's just a bite — just physical."

VI.
The Precipice

The Precipice

How it looked from the precipice.

No destination out of sight,
My castle in the air only a stone's throw away,
And the key to the door ringing in the forge.

Every imperfection was sacred.
Some otherworldly alignment set it that way and I could see all the connections.

My mind fired with a supernatural capacity.

Neural networks overclocked,
A bonfire of the spirit and soul.

Then it went too far — the river met the sea.

The intersection opened and I was higher than any angel,
A vessel for something greater.

Impossibly chaotic to sustain or reason with.

Something beyond human.

www.ingramcontent.com/pod-product-compliance
Lightning Source LLC
Chambersburg PA
CBHW032338300426
44109CB00041B/1284